Smart Dog

by Kirsten Anderson
illustrated by Nicole Wong

Editorial Offices: Glenview, Illinois • Parsippany, New Jersey • New York, New York
Sales Offices: Needham, Massachusetts • Duluth, Georgia • Glenview, Illinois
Coppell, Texas • Ontario, California • Mesa, Arizona

Every effort has been made to secure permission and provide appropriate credit for photographic material. The publisher deeply regrets any omission and pledges to correct errors called to its attention in subsequent editions.

Unless otherwise acknowledged, all photographs are the property of Scott Foresman, a division of Pearson Education.

Photo locators denoted as follows: Top (T), Center (C), Bottom (B), Left (L), Right (R), Background (Bkgd)

Illustrations by Nicole Wong

ISBN: 0-328-13381-7

Copyright © Pearson Education, Inc.

All Rights Reserved. Printed in the United States of America. This publication is protected by Copyright, and permission should be obtained from the publisher prior to any prohibited reproduction, storage in a retrieval system, or transmission in any form by any means, electronic, mechanical, photocopying, recording, or likewise. For information regarding permission(s), write to: Permissions Department, Scott Foresman, 1900 East Lake Avenue, Glenview, Illinois 60025.

4 5 6 7 8 9 10 V0G1 14 13 12 11 10 09 08 07 06

"Sit, Toby!" Charlie commanded. He held his breath and watched his dog, Toby. They had worked on the sit command yesterday, and Charlie hoped that the dog would remember the lesson.

Toby wagged his silky tail and panted excitedly. *Maybe Charlie wants to give me a treat,* he thought. Toby skipped forward and pressed his nose against Charlie's knees, nudging him.

Charlie sighed, "No, Toby. That's not *sit*. That's *walk*."

"Sit!" Charlie said again, as he tried to push Toby into a sitting position. Toby flopped down lazily and rolled over to have his stomach scratched.

"Are you still trying to train that silly dog?" Charlie turned around and saw his sister Eileen standing on the porch.

"He's not silly," Charlie said. "We're working very hard on a new trick."

Eileen laughed. "A new trick? He doesn't know *any* tricks. I'll bet he doesn't even know his own name. You won't be able to teach him anything, Charlie. Come on. It's your turn to set the table for dinner."

"Oh, really? I guarantee that Toby can learn anything," Charlie said. "If Toby can do a trick that he's learned, will you promise to stop calling him a silly dog?"

"How about this?" Eileen asked. "If you can teach him a trick in one week, I'll set the table and wash and dry the dishes every night for a week. If you can't teach him, then you'll do all three chores for a week."

"Deal," Charlie agreed.

"I can't wait to have my week off from chores," teased Eileen. As she turned to go inside, she said, "By the way, your silly dog is digging up Mom's flowers."

Charlie pulled Toby away from the garden and frantically tried to push the dirt back into place so Mom wouldn't notice.

It had taken a long time for Mom and Dad to decide that he could have a dog. Charlie had promised that he would take care of the dog all by himself. Finally, they agreed, and the family made the trip to the animal shelter.

The people at the shelter introduced them to all kinds of dogs. Charlie liked them all and didn't know which one to choose, but then four puppies scampered into the room. They played and tumbled over each other until one bounded out of the pack, ran straight to Charlie, and began licking his hand.

Charlie knew right away that that puppy was the one he wanted. Charlie and Toby had been best friends ever since, and training Toby had become Charlie's biggest goal.

Charlie finished replanting the tulips, and now he needed to get back to work with Toby. One week seemed like a short time to teach him to sit, especially when he was more interested in digging up Mom's flowers.

"Toby, sit!" Charlie commanded again.

Toby ran around in a circle. He thought Charlie wanted to play one of their games, but he didn't know which one. He tried jumping up on Charlie, but he sensed that Charlie wasn't happy. Toby wanted to please Charlie, but he wasn't sure how to do it. He stood beside the boy and licked his hand.

"Don't worry, Toby," Charlie said, brightening as he patted his dog's head. We'll figure out how to show everyone just how smart you really are."

The next day, Charlie rode his bike to the library and looked for books about dog training. He found one that promised to reveal secrets of dog trainers who worked with animals on TV.

Charlie checked the book out of the library and began reading as soon as he got home. According to the book, Toby needed clear commands and instant rewards of praise and treats. Charlie filled his pockets with biscuits and led Toby outside into the backyard.

"Sit!" Charlie said firmly in a loud voice. But instead of sitting, Toby barked and ran towards Charlie. Charlie tried to push Toby into a sitting position while holding a biscuit above his nose. Toby was so excited by the scent of the biscuit that he jumped up to grab it with his mouth.

Charlie's friend Nina came to visit the next day, and she had an idea about how to train Toby. "Your words don't mean anything to him," she explained. "He needs an example to follow."

"What do you mean?" Charlie asked.

"I'll give the command, and you act like a dog and obey my command," Nina said. "Then I'll give you a treat, and you can pretend to gobble it up. Toby will watch you, and then he'll understand that he'll get a treat if he does the trick too."

"It sounds silly, Nina, but I guess it's worth a try," Charlie said.

Charlie and Nina went into the house to get some dog treats for Toby. Nina hid the treats in her pocket as they walked back out to the backyard. Toby sniffed and twitched his nose. He smelled dog biscuits.

"Sit!" Nina commanded loudly and clearly. She gestured to Charlie, pointing to the ground. Charlie sighed and slowly did his best imitation of an obedient, sitting dog. Nina came over to him and held out a treat. "Good boy!" Nina praised Charlie. She clapped her hands and patted Charlie's head.

Charlie pretended to chew the biscuit. He watched Toby out of the corner of his eye. Toby was staring at the biscuit. *Maybe this will work*, Charlie thought. But when Nina gave the sit command again, instead of sitting, Toby raced forward and jumped on Nina. He stuck his nose into her pocket. Nina fell backwards, and Toby trotted away happily, holding two biscuits in his mouth.

Nina looked at Charlie and said with a smile, "He's smart enough to find the biscuits!"

The next morning Toby ran out into the backyard. He sniffed the air and noticed an interesting scent coming from the flowers—or maybe it was coming from underneath the flowers! Toby's nose twitched, and he raced to the flower bed to investigate the smell. Dirt began to fly as he busily dug, until he heard Mom shout, "No, Toby! No!"

"I know this dirt is very inviting," Charlie told Toby as he shoveled the dirt back into the flower bed, "but you have to stop digging in it!"

Toby slunk under the porch and watched Charlie replant the flowers. He felt sad that Mom yelled, and he decided that he should stay away from the flowers from now on.

The week was almost over, and Toby hadn't learned a trick yet. That afternoon, Charlie filled his pockets with biscuits and headed out to the backyard. Toby trotted happily behind him and lay down on the grass. He liked being with Charlie.

"Maybe *sit* isn't the right trick for you right now," Charlie said. "Let's try something else today. Stay, Toby!" Charlie said. He put his hand on Toby's back and held him in place. Then he let go and stepped away from the dog. Toby began to stand, but Charlie walked back and held him still again.

"Stay," he said firmly. Charlie backed away slowly. *It's working*, he thought excitedly. Toby lay still and watched Charlie. He smelled a biscuit.

"Good Toby! Good boy!" Charlie cheered. Toby wagged his tail happily. He was glad that Charlie was happy, and he hoped that he would get the biscuit. Suddenly, a quick movement in the bushes drew Toby's attention away from the biscuit. It was a squirrel! Toby jumped up, barked loudly, and raced across the backyard, away from Charlie. He heard Charlie calling him, but he wanted to chase the squirrel more than he wanted to obey Charlie. The gate in the fence was open, and Toby ran through the opening and into the front yard.

Charlie was horrified. Toby was not supposed to go out of the backyard. It was too dangerous to be in the front of the house where he could reach the street.

"Toby, come back!" Charlie yelled as he raced after the swift dog.

Toby ran through Mrs. Farrell's yard next door. Then he made his way into Mr. Smith's backyard, where he found himself face to face with a cat. The cat hissed at him, and Toby darted away quickly. He ran through more yards. He lost the scent of the squirrel but quickly picked up other smells. In one yard, he ran after a robin, and in another, he chased a chipmunk. He even smelled dogs in some yards, though he didn't see any. All of these scents were new and interesting to Toby, and he had forgotten all about the squirrel.

Charlie ran down the street, calling Toby. When he didn't see his dog anywhere, he ran back home and told Mom what had happened. She came outside to help.

"Don't worry," she said, "we'll find him."

Toby was tired of running, so he lay down to rest on some cool dirt in the shade. Then he remembered the biscuit and decided to find Charlie. He sniffed the air, lowered his nose to the ground, and began to follow his own scent back along the path he had taken. This time, though, he avoided Mr. Smith's cat.

Charlie and his mother had been walking up and down the street for half an hour. They had called Toby's name, and they had asked their neighbors if they had seen him, but no one had. Charlie began to lose hope when, suddenly, he saw a familiar shape at the end of the street. "Toby!" Charlie cried.

Toby's ears perked up. He knew that *he* was Toby and that Charlie was calling *him*. Then he spotted Charlie running down the street toward him. He ran and leapt into Charlie's arms, almost knocking Charlie over. He hoped Charlie still had the biscuit.

Charlie hugged him joyfully. "You came home all by yourself, Toby! Good boy! Smart dog!"

Later that afternoon, Charlie relaxed in his room while Toby slept next to him in his dog bed on the floor.

"I heard Toby ran away," Eileen said as she poked her head through the doorway.

Charlie nodded. "The gate was open," he said. "We all have to be careful and make sure it's latched from now on."

"I'll be very careful," Eileen said, sitting down next to Toby and patting him softly.

Suddenly, Charlie had a new thought. "Hey! I won our bet!" he exclaimed. "Toby found his way home, and that counts as a trick! Right?"

Eileen shrugged. "That's just instinct," she said. "All dogs can find their way home. You guaranteed that Toby would perform a trick that he had *learned*."

"I know," Charlie sighed. He imagined setting the table *and* washing and drying the dishes for the next week. Then he had an idea. "Wait a minute!" he said. "Toby answered to his name! That's not instinct. That's something that he actually learned!"

"Really?" asked Eileen, looking at him suspiciously. "Prove it."

"Watch this," Charlie said. "Toby! Toby!" he called. Toby snored, and Charlie shook him gently.

"Hey! That's cheating!" Eileen complained. "You're waking him up, and that's not the same thing as Toby answering to his name."

"How can he answer if he's asleep?" Charlie questioned his sister. "Come on, Toby. Toby!"

Toby opened his eyes and stared at Charlie. Then he yawned and fell back asleep with his front paws tucked beneath his chin.

"Look," said Eileen, "let's just forget about our deal, all right? You don't have to do all the chores next week. I guess finding his way home is a pretty good trick, even if all dogs can do it."

"Thanks," said Charlie. "I won't give up though. You'll see that Toby will learn lots of things. We just need more time."

Eileen shrugged. "That's all right. I'm glad he's home, even if he is just a silly dog."

She left the room, closing the door quietly behind her. Toby was snoring, and Charlie turned around and patted his head.

Toby twitched his paws and kicked his legs. He was dreaming about chasing the squirrel, but this time it was different. In his dream, he barked when the cat hissed at him, and the cat ran away.

Just as Toby was about to catch the squirrel in his dream, he woke up. He jumped up and pranced to the other side of the room. Then he walked slowly in a circle, shaking his head.

Charlie laughed and asked, "What were you dreaming about, Toby?"

Toby heard his name, turned around, and trotted straight over to Charlie.

"Toby!" Charlie cried excitedly. "You *do* know your name! You *learned* it!" He reached down and rubbed Toby's ears. Toby licked Charlie's face and hands. Then Charlie commanded, "Toby, sit!"

Toby paused for a few seconds. The word *sit* sounded familiar, and he thought about the biscuit he had been wishing for. Then he sat.

Charlie was amazed! "Good dog! Good Toby!" he cried happily as he hugged his dog. "I knew you could do it! You're a smart dog! You can learn anything!"

Best of Show

If you love dogs, the Westminster Kennel Club Dog Show is the show for you! It's the most famous judging event for dogs in the world. The show is held every February in New York City.

At the show, dogs are groomed and shown by their "handlers." Handlers are men and women hired by the dogs' owners to train the dogs and make them look their best.

The judges look for the dog that has all the best qualities. They feel the dogs' coats and bones, look in their mouths to check their teeth, and watch them as they walk or trot with their handlers.

Many of the dogs are like actors. They like to perform for the crowd.

After two days of competition, one dog is chosen as "Best in Show." The winner receives a big silver trophy and appears on TV news shows the next day!